I LOVE ISRAEL

I LOVE ISRAEL

CAROLE AYRES

Crippled Beagle Publishing

This work is protected by the copyright laws of the United States of America. No part of this book may be reproduced or stored, in whole or in part, in print or digital format, without express permission by the author. For information regarding permission, interviews, events, and quotes, write to the publisher.

Crippled Beagle Publishing
5413 Glen Cove Drive, Knoxville, Tennessee 37919

©2018 by Carole Ayres. All rights reserved.

Photo credits: Carole Ayres, Annie Ayres, and Martha Ann Fulk

Scroll image: SaimGraphics Digital Art / Drawings & Paintings / Still Life
saimgraphics.deviantart.com

Candle image: Pixabay, pixabay.com

Mount Sinai image: https://www.flickr.com/photos/27718315@N02/4809330547/

Book design by Jody Dyer

ISBN-13: 978-1-970037-05-0

Dear reader,

Come along with me to see the Sinai Peninsula where Moses received the Ten Commandments from God. The Israelites stayed at the base of Mount Sinai waiting for Moses' return. On this trip we ride camels and dance while dressed in fancy garb. Early in the morning, we hike to the top of Mount Sinai and watch the sun rise over this Holy Place.

Then on we go to Jerusalem, the Holy City. We stop to ponder a 2,000-year-old tree in Gethsemane under which Jesus may have prayed the night before he died. We ride on a boat like those that carried Jesus and His disciples. We watch a fisherman cast his net. Finally, we spend time at the Temple Mount and ponder the significance of this Holy site for so many Christians, Muslims, and Jews. I hope you will go there some day to see this beautiful place.

Carole Ayres
קרול איירס

For Caroline קרוליין, Charlie צ'רלי, Sadie סיידי, Carson קרסון, Campbell קמפבל, Kade קייד, and Keegan קיגן

On the way to Israel,
We stopped at Mount Sinai.
It was here the Israelites,
Let forty years go by.

We looked at the pyramids and took a camel ride.
The challenge was to not let the camels collide.

After jiggles and bumps,
We rode in the sand.
At the base of Mount Sinai,
We made a great plan.

We belly danced and sang like the Israelites.
We laughed at ourselves and said our goodnights.

Our goal was to arrive,
At sunrise to see,
Where God gave Ten Commandments to Moses,
For you and for me.

People from all over the world headed to the top,
Singing in different languages, we had to stop.

We sang in English.
It felt so grand,
The sun rising, all those people,
God's flawless plan!

Then off to the Sea of Galilee,
We went to explore,
We climbed into a boat,
To hear what was in store.

The American flag was raised as we sang,
For "The Star Spangled Banner" my heart felt a pang.
I was overwhelmed with national pride,
To see in Galilee our flag and Israel's,
Flying side by side.

Stories were shared about Jesus on the sea,
And how being there made it so real; We all agreed.
To enhance our visions, a fisherman threw out his net.
Imagining Jesus with us, we did not regret.

We touched a 2,000-year-old olive tree.
We thought about Jesus,
In prayer on His knees.

It was here Jesus thought of us and wept,
Then prayed, "Father, Your plan I accept."

Next, to Jerusalem we went to see,
The way of the cross,
Where Jesus gained heaven for you and me.
We encouraged each other again and again,
To pray for all peoples, this world to mend.

At last we stood before the Dome of the Rock.
The Holy place to which three religions flock.
The location is claimed by Muslims, Christians, and Jews,
To be holy and unique to their very own faiths' views.

And so, dear reader,
I thank you again,
For joining me to see,
This Holy Land!

About the Author

Carole Ayres (right) grew up in Tennessee and resides there with her husband Joe and their three sons, two daughters-in-law, and seven grandchildren. Carole is a retired teacher. She tutors English language learners in her son's third grade math class. With her family, Carole enjoys spending time outdoors—from hiking the Great Smoky Mountains and boating Douglas Lake in Tennessee, to skiing Colorado slopes or exploring the beaches of Turks and Caicos. Carole is a world-traveler who loves sharing her passion for discovery with young people.

Look for other *I LOVE* books by Carole Ayres on Amazon.com, Kindle, Barnes & Noble, and other retailers. For information on future titles, book signings, quotes, excerpts, and interviews, write to:

Crippled Beagle Publishing, 5413 Glen Cove Drive
Knoxville, Tennessee 37919
dyer.cbpublishing@gmail.com

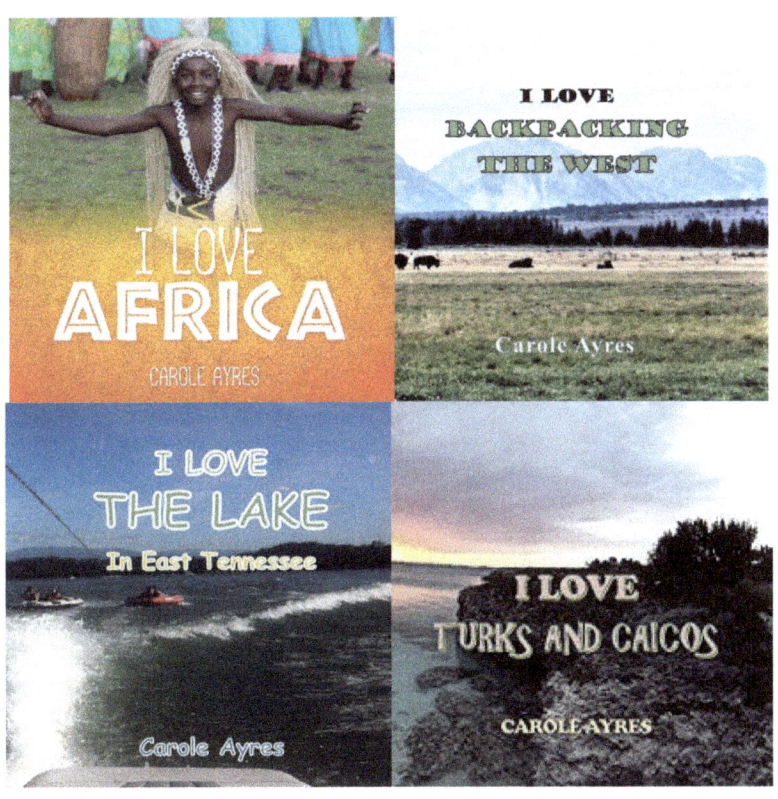

www.ingramcontent.com/pod-product-compliance
Lightning Source LLC
Chambersburg PA
CBHW040011080526
44586CB00028B/2965